E-voting in Nigeria can be a su

By

Dr. Alex Ndukwe

First printing, 2019

Printed in the United States of America

ISBN: 978-0-359-82630-8

Dedication

This book is dedicated to his Excellency, Gen. Muhammadu Buhari (GCFR) President, Federal Republic of Nigeria for his integrity and fight against corruption, a deadly virus that has remained in our society for ages.

Acknowledgement

I wish to appreciate my LinkedIn contact and friend, Evans Nwawuefe for his support during this book project.

TABLE OF CONTENTS

Forward

Electronic voting has revolutionized electoral process in countries like brazil, India, Estonia etc. web based solutions has experienced lots of setbacks characterized with hacking, intrusion and this would allow cyber criminals to manipulate results and this led to some countries putting a hold on it for now , Microsoft is set to launch a more secured system that would be used in United states for 2020 elections.

Our country is peculiar considering internet penetration & infrastructural gap that has ravaged our rural areas, a solution that would not involve internet service, electricity etc. should meet our needs across the wards nationwide.

The author has described this M3 equipment which some African countries like Namibia & Kenya are planning to acquire. Electoral process should not encourage waste of public funds, results that lacks credibility, integrity and most importantly litigations at tribunals all the time after elections.

Voters participation will increase, this concept will herald integrity, improved process, voters do not need to waste too much time at the pollen units and results will be released within 24 hours.

We have enjoyed 20 years of uninterrupted democracy, let's ensure we make our polls free and fair, ensuring the vote of the electorate counts.

Introduction

"We can no longer continue to conduct elections manually in Nigeria; we must introduce modern technology as is being done in other countries ....Very soon the use of technology for the conduct of local elections in the country will be mandatory".

Prof. Mahmood Yakubu (INEC chairman).

(INEC to adopt electronic voting in 2019,daily post newspaper, may 25 2016)

Nigeria for the past twenty years has enjoyed uninterrupted democracy. Despite this, conducting a credible election has been a challenge in Nigeria, often elections are bewildered with irregularities and it has become a norm that results are challenged at election tribunals, most times winners are declared in the courts. What this implies is that there is an urgent need to improve on the card reader device that was introduced in the 2015 general elections by Prof. Attahiru Jega the then Chairman of Independent National Electoral Commission

(INEC), this was aimed at ensuring that voters are authenticated before they cast their votes.

On the other hand, Nigeria is seen as one of the lowest broadband penetration rates among countries in the world. Many parts of the country cannot boast of a good network for phone calls, let alone access to the Internet. Also, the issue of hacking is so problematic that some countries which adopted electronic voting in their electoral processes have since discontinued or suspended it. INEC's focus should not be only providing technology, but should also been on investigating its effective management, maintenance and availability during elections. It should also focus on mechanisms to solve issues that may arise after the conduct of the elections.

INEC needs to be commended for the smooth provision of logistics during the 2019 general elections; materials got to rural areas in good time, delays were only experienced in very few locations and thus, it can only get better. This notwithstanding, INEC performed woefully in the distribution of Permanent Voters' Card (PVC) cards, lots of cards were not distributed and despite strategies adopted to ensure voters receive them. An opportunity to continue with the distribution of the PVC is here now that the elections are over.

Most democracies in the world often have credible elections, cases of rigging or irregularities are rarely heard, Nigeria needs to borrow a leaf from them in this direction, India with about 300 political parties participating in their elections rarely has issues with election malpractices, this is because elections are done via electronic voting. A political analyst in Nigeria once said that the political parties in Nigeria should be reduced. this is not basically the problem of the Nigerian electoral system, there is need to think outside the box and bring in the use of technology to strengthen the process, if this can be achieved, the issue of electoral violence and malpractices will be a thing of the past.

One challenge is the infrastructure gap in Nigeria, there is need to bridge the technological infrastructural gap between the urban areas with the rural areas. Also voter orientation should be carried out in the rural areas (especially on the use of technology in the election process) nevertheless electronic voting should be the target during the next general election and the time for INEC to swing into action is now, there is no point waiting till a year before the elections.

The June 12, 1993 elections was adjudged the most credible elections in the history of Nigeria, the option A4 was adopted by the then National Electoral Commission (NEC) helmsman, Prof. Humphrey Nwosu. The method adjoined to be very successful; this point to the fact that technology is not the only requirement but an effective process is also an essential component for success. Box snatching, massive rigging, vote buying and other election malpractices is very common with all elections conducted during first to fourth republic and there is need to be sure that technologies will not be hijacked during elections as well.

This book will review the challenges and proffer suggestions that will lead to more credible elections while taking into consideration other challenges like security, logistics and personnel.

There is need for Nigeria to appreciate the fact that electronic voting system is adopted in many countries. Nations like Brazil, Australia, Malaysia, United States, and others has adopted the system. Although these countries are also faced with challenges, the system is more convenient in terms of ballot and collation of results.

Before Nigeria can transit into such systems, there must be an amendment of the electoral policy in the constitution of Federal Republic of Nigeria thus, will justify the use of technology in the electoral process. This will give the country respect when it comes to elections and democratic values will be entrenched in Nigeria.

The use of electronic voting in elections remains a contentious issue. Some countries such as Netherlands and Germany have stopped using it after it was shown to be unreliable, while the Indian Election commission recommends it. The involvement of numerous stakeholders including companies that manufacture these machines as well as political parties that stand to gain from rigging complicates this further.

It is very evident that the stakeholders are the ones that will make it a success, if they are negative about it, definitely it will not see the light of the day. Many stakeholders might feel that since the card readers are problematic, electronic approach to elections may crash and possibly negate the gains recorded, but there is a need to continue to improve as a nation.

The security of electronic voting machines is almost entirely dependent on the implementation of security protocols at each locality. According to a recent research on the Estonian elections, massive operational lapses in security from transferring election results on personal thumb drives to posting network credentials on the wall in view of the public. The researchers concluded that these systems are insecure in their current implementation, and due to the rise of nation state interest in influencing elections, should be "discontinued".

From my assessment, no system is 100% perfect, apologies to mechanical engineers, efficiency of machines is pegged at 70% and one can understand that we cannot have an efficiency of 100% , we must strive against all odds to achieve this and I believe it's attainable.

Database hackers might see the innovation as an opportunity to work for dubious politicians so as to manipulate the system, there is need to note that I.T. security solutions are available so as to prevent unauthorized intrusion into the database, there is no cause for alarm, stakeholders must be conscious of this, rigging could still take place if there are no proactive measures with respect to authenticity of the data being generated.

Other school of thought might also assert that Nigeria's democracy is not advanced yet, why go for electronic voting, let's continue with the manual system, demographics might even come into play and we might also want to say that rural areas are not literate enough to use this systems to be provided, INEC would have to step up with voters education in vernacular and many more issues will still arise.

A worthy e-voting system must perform most of these tasks while complying with a set of standards established by regulatory bodies, and must also be capable to deal successfully with strong requirements associated with security, accuracy, integrity, swiftness, privacy, audit-ability, accessibility, cost-effectiveness, scalability and ecological sustainability.

Obviously, there is need to look at the cost of organizing an election in Nigeria, my opinion, it's outrageous and we must shop for most effective options so as to eliminate wastes of resources.

Nigeria's elections are among the most expensive in the world, with the cost soaring from a little above N1 billion in 1999 to over N100 billion in 2015 while the 2019 general elections costing N69 billon more than the previous election ,investigations by Daily Trust has shown. The country's huge cost of elections has surpassed that of the world's largest democracy, India, with a population six times bigger than Nigeria's.

Nigeria, with 67 million registered voters, spent $625 million during the 2015 elections, translating into $9.33 per voter, according to data prepared by the National Institute for Legislative Studies (NILS) in 2015.This figure is higher than the $600 million the Electoral Commission of India (ECI) said it spent during the 2014 general elections in which 553.8 million people voted out of 815 million registered voters.

Nigeria's $625 million was spent in funding expenditure that included information technology systems and infrastructure; maps and voter lists preparation; training for returning officers, field staff and special events staff, the NILS data said.

S/N	Year	Voter Registration	Days For Registration	Data Captured	D-Base	Accreditation/ Voting	Result Collation
1	1999	Pen/Sheets and Typewriters	14 Days	Basic details. no picture or finger prints	NIL	NIL	NIL
2	2003	Optical Magnetic Recognition Form (Omr Form) *Automated Finger Prints Identification System (Afis)	10 Days	Basic details and finger prints only	YES	NIL	NIL
3	2007	*Direct Data Capture Machine (Ddcm) * (Afis)	4 Months	Basic details, photograph, and finger prints	YES	Electronic Voters' Register (EVR)	Excel Sheet/E-mail
4	2011	*Direct Data Capture Machine (Ddcm) * Afis	21 Days	Basic details, photograph, and finger prints	YES	Electronic Voters' Register (EVR)	Excel Sheet/E-mail
5	2015	*Direct Data Capture Machine (Ddcm) *Improved Afis/Business Rule.	Continuous Voters Registration (CVR)	Basic details, photograph, and finger prints	YES	* EVR *INEC Voters Authentication System (IVAS)/Smart Card Reader (SCR)	Election Transparency Administration And Collation (e-TRAC)
6	2016	* Ddcm *Improved Afis *Business Rule.	Continuous Voters Registration (CVR)	Basic details, photograph, and finger prints	YES	*EVR *IVAS	*Electronic Collation Support (E-Collation) * e-TRAC

Source: American Journal of computer science & information Technology

The table above reveals that we have only deployed technology for voters data capture and authenticity of voters , collation was done manually and this takes a lot of time , results takes a lot of time and I believe we can achieve more feats as a nation by adopting a simple and effective approach that will eliminate thuggery, rigging, manipulations etc.

Chapter 1
Challenges of Electoral Process

There are enormous challenges in organizing an election in Nigeria using the manual process and we must appreciate the efforts of the election umpire INEC , though there is need to acknowledge that issues bothering on logistics, accessing rural areas with ease, funding in good time, managing adopted technologies – Card reader for authenticating voters are still confronting the commission.

According to a democratic index carried out by "The Economist", a United-Kingdom (UK) based company with the intention of measuring the state of democracy in 167 countries, of which 166 are sovereign states and 164 are United Nations (UN) member states. The index was first published in 2006, with updates for 2008, 2010 and later years.

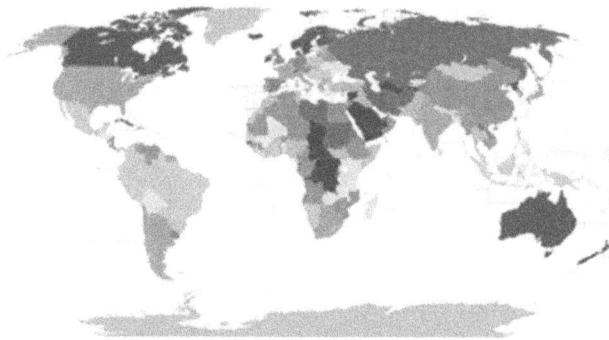

Full democracies Flawed democracies Hybrid regimes Authoritarian regimes
9.01–10   7.01–8   5.01–6   3.01–4
8.01–9   6.01–7   4.01–5   2.01–3
                                               0–2

The Economist Intelligence Unit Democracy Index map for 2018.

The index is based on 60 indicators grouped in five different categories, measuring pluralism, civil liberties and political culture. In addition to a numeric score and a ranking; The index categorises each country in one of four regime types: full democracies, flawed democracies, hybrid regimes and authoritarian regimes.

Nigeria is ranked number 108 out of 167 countries with 4.44 points as a Hybrid regime, this can improve with good processes in place and this would come alive with electronic voting. let's look at the table below

Democracy Index 2018

Rank	Country	Score	Electoral process and plura-lism	Functio-ning of govern-ment	Poli-tical partici-pation	Poli-tical culture	Civil liber-ties	Regime type
1	Norway	9.87	10	9.64	10	10	9.71	Full democracy
2	Iceland	9.58	10	9.29	8.89	10	9.71	Full democracy
3	Sweden	9.39	9.58	9.64	8.33	10	9.41	Full democracy
4	New Zealand	9.26	10	9.29	8.89	8.13	10	Full democracy
5	Denmark	9.22	10	9.29	8.33	9.38	9.12	Full democracy
6	Ireland	9.15	9.58	7.86	8.33	10	10	Full democracy
6	Canada	9.15	9.58	9.64	7.78	8.75	10	Full democracy
8	Finland	9.14	10	8.93	8.33	8.75	9.71	Full democracy
9	Australia	9.09	10	8.93	7.78	8.75	10	Full democracy
10	Switzerland	9.03	9.58	9.29	7.78	9.38	9.12	Full democracy
11	Netherlands	8.89	9.58	9.29	8.33	8.13	9.12	Full democracy
12	Luxembourg	8.81	10	8.93	6.67	8.75	9.71	Full democracy
13	Germany	8.68	9.58	8.57	8.33	7.5	9.41	Full democracy
14	United Kingdom	8.53	9.58	7.5	8.33	8.13	9.12	Full democracy
15	Uruguay	8.38	10	8.57	6.11	7.5	9.71	Full democracy
16	Austria	8.29	9.58	7.86	8.33	6.88	8.82	Full democracy
17	Mauritius	8.22	9.17	8.21	5.56	8.75	9.41	Full democracy
18	Malta	8.21	9.17	8.21	6.11	8.75	8.82	Full democracy

19	Spain	8.08	9.17	7.14	7.78	7.5	8.82	Full democracy
20	Costa Rica	8.07	9.58	7.5	6.67	7.5	9.12	Full democracy
21	South Korea	8	9.17	7.86	7.22	7.5	8.24	Flawed democracy[a]
22	Japan	7.99	8.75	8.21	6.67	7.5	8.82	Flawed democracy
23	Chile	7.97	9.58	8.57	4.44	8.13	9.12	Flawed democracy
	Estonia	7.97	9.58	8.21	6.67	6.88	8.53	Flawed democracy
25	United States	7.96	9.17	7.14	7.78	7.5	8.24	Flawed democracy
26	Cape Verde	7.88	9.17	7.86	6.67	6.88	8.82	Flawed democracy
27	Portugal	7.84	9.58	7.5	6.11	6.88	9.12	Flawed democracy
28	Botswana	7.81	9.17	7.14	6.11	7.5	9.12	Flawed democracy
29	France	7.8	9.58	7.5	7.78	5.63	8.53	Flawed democracy
30	Israel	7.79	9.17	7.5	8.89	7.5	5.88	Flawed democracy
31	Belgium	7.78	9.58	8.93	5	6.88	8.53	Flawed democracy
32	Taiwan	7.73	9.58	8.21	6.11	5.63	9.12	Flawed democracy
33	Italy	7.71	9.58	6.07	7.78	6.88	8.24	Flawed democracy
34	Czech Republic	7.69	9.58	6.79	6.67	6.88	8.53	Flawed democracy
35	Cyprus	7.59	9.17	6.43	6.67	6.88	8.82	Flawed democracy
36	Slovenia	7.5	9.58	6.79	6.67	6.25	8.24	Flawed democracy
	Lithuania	7.5	9.58	6.43	6.11	6.25	9.12	Flawed democracy
38	Latvia	7.38	9.58	6.07	5.56	6.88	8.82	Flawed democracy

39	Greece	7.29	9.58	5.36	6.11	6.88	8.53	Flawed democracy
40	South Africa	7.24	7.42	7.5	8.33	5	7.94	Flawed democracy
41	India	7.23	9.17	6.79	7.22	5.63	7.35	Flawed democracy
42	Timor-Leste	7.19	9.08	6.79	5.56	6.88	7.65	Flawed democracy
43	Trinidad and Tobago	7.16	9.58	7.14	6.11	5.63	7.35	Flawed democracy
44	Slovakia	7.1	9.58	6.79	5.56	5.63	7.94	Flawed democracy
45	Panama	7.05	9.58	6.07	6.67	5	7.94	Flawed democracy
46	Bulgaria	7.03	9.17	6.43	7.22	4.38	7.94	Flawed democracy
47	Argentina	7.02	9.17	5.36	6.11	6.25	8.24	Flawed democracy
	Jamaica	7.02	8.75	7.14	4.44	6.25	8.53	Flawed democracy
49	Suriname	6.98	9.17	6.43	6.67	5	7.65	Flawed democracy
50	Brazil	6.97	9.58	5.36	6.67	5	8.24	Flawed democracy
51	Colombia	6.96	9.17	6.79	5	5.63	8.24	Flawed democracy
52	Malaysia	6.88	7.75	7.86	6.67	6.25	5.88	Flawed democracy
53	Philippines	6.71	9.17	5.71	7.22	4.38	7.06	Flawed democracy
54	Poland	6.67	9.17	6.07	6.11	4.38	7.65	Flawed democracy
	Guyana	6.67	9.17	5.71	6.11	5	7.35	Flawed democracy
56	Lesotho	6.64	9.17	5	6.67	5.63	6.76	Flawed democracy
57	Ghana	6.63	8.33	5.71	6.67	6.25	6.18	Flawed democracy
	Hungary	6.63	8.75	6.07	5	6.25	7.06	Flawed democracy

59	Peru	6.6	9.17	5	5.56	5.63	7.65	Flawed democracy
60	Croatia	6.57	9.17	6.07	5.56	5	7.06	Flawed democracy
61	Dominican Republic	6.54	9.17	5.36	6.11	5	7.06	Flawed democracy
62	Mongolia	6.5	9.17	5.71	5.56	5	7.06	Flawed democracy
63	Serbia	6.41	8.25	5.36	6.11	5	7.35	Flawed democracy
	Tunisia	6.41	6.42	5.71	7.78	6.25	5.88	Flawed democracy
65	Indonesia	6.39	6.92	7.14	6.67	5.63	5.59	Flawed democracy
66	Singapore	6.38	4.33	7.86	6.11	6.25	7.35	Flawed democracy
	Romania	6.38	9.17	5.71	5	4.38	7.65	Flawed democracy
68	Ecuador	6.27	8.75	5.36	6.11	4.38	6.76	Flawed democracy
69	Namibia	6.25	5.67	5.36	6.67	5.63	7.94	Flawed democracy
70	Paraguay	6.24	8.75	5.71	5	4.38	7.35	Flawed democracy
71	Sri Lanka	6.19	7.83	5.71	5	6.25	6.18	Flawed democracy
	Mexico	6.19	8.33	6.07	7.22	3.13	6.18	Flawed democracy
73	Hong Kong	6.15	3.08	6.07	5.56	7.5	8.53	Flawed democracy
	Senegal	6.15	7.5	6.07	4.44	6.25	6.47	Flawed democracy
75	Papua New Guinea	6.03	6.92	6.07	3.89	5.63	7.65	Flawed democracy
76	Albania	5.98	7	4.71	5.56	5	7.65	Hybrid regime
77	Salvador	5.96	9.17	4.29	5.56	3.75	7.06	Hybrid regime
78	North Macedonia	5.87	6.5	5.36	6.67	3.75	7.06	Hybrid regime
79	Moldova	5.85	7.08	4.64	6.11	4.38	7.06	Hybrid regime
	Fiji	5.85	6.58	5.36	6.11	5.63	5.59	Hybrid regime
81	Montenegro	5.74	6.08	5.36	6.11	4.38	6.76	Hybrid regime
	Benin	5.74	6.5	5.71	5	5.63	5.88	Hybrid regime
83	Bolivia	5.7	7.5	4.64	5.56	3.75	7.06	Hybrid regime

84	Ukraine	5.69	6.17	3.21	6.67	6.25	6.18 Hybrid regime
85	Honduras	5.63	8.5	4.64	4.44	4.38	6.18 Hybrid regime
86	Zambia	5.61	6.17	4.64	3.89	6.88	6.47 Hybrid regime
87	Guatemala	5.6	7.92	5.36	3.89	4.38	6.47 Hybrid regime
88	Banglad esh	5.57	7.83	5.07	5.56	4.38	5 Hybrid regime
89	Georgia	5.5	7.83	3.57	6.11	4.38	5.59 Hybrid regime
90	Malawi	5.49	6.58	4.29	4.44	6.25	5.88 Hybrid regime
91	Tanzania	5.41	7	5	5	5.63	4.41 Hybrid regime
	Mali	5.41	7.42	3.93	3.89	5.63	6.18 Hybrid regime
93	Liberia	5.35	7.42	2.57	5.56	5.63	5.59 Hybrid regime
94	Bhutan	5.3	8.75	6.79	2.78	4.38	3.82 Hybrid regime
95	Madagas car	5.22	6.08	3.57	6.11	5.63	4.71 Hybrid regime
96	Uganda	5.2	5.25	3.57	4.44	6.88	5.88 Hybrid regime
97	Nepal	5.18	4.33	5.36	5	5.63	5.59 Hybrid regime
98	Kenya	5.11	3.5	5.36	6.67	5.63	4.41 Hybrid regime
	Kyrgyzst an	5.11	6.58	2.93	6.67	4.38	5 Hybrid regime
100	Morocco	4.99	5.25	4.64	5	5.63	4.41 Hybrid regime
101	Bosnia and Herzegov ina	4.98	6.5	2.93	5.56	3.75	6.18 Hybrid regime
102	Haiti	4.91	5.58	2.93	3.89	6.25	5.88 Hybrid regime

103	Armenia	**4.79**	5.67	4.64	5.56	2.5	5.59 Hybrid regime
104	rkina Faso	**4.75**	4.42	4.29	4.44	5.63	5 Hybrid regime
105	rra Leone	**4.66**	6.58	1.86	3.33	6.25	5.29 Hybrid regime
106	Lebanon	**4.63**	3.92	2.21	6.67	5.63	4.71 Hybrid regime
	Thailand	**4.63**	3	4.29	5	5	5.88 Hybrid regime
108	Nigeria	**4.44**	6.08	4.64	3.33	3.75	4.41 Hybrid regime
109	Palestine	**4.39**	3.83	2.14	7.78	4.38	3.82 Hybrid regime
110	Turkey	**4.37**	4.5	5	5	5	2.35 Hybrid regime
111	Gambia	**4.31**	4.48	4.29	3.33	5.63	3.82 Hybrid regime
112	Pakistan	**4.17**	6.08	5.36	2.22	2.5	4.71 Hybrid regime
113	ory Coast	**4.15**	4.83	2.86	3.33	5.63	4.12 Hybrid regime
114	Iraq	**4.06**	4.75	0.07	6.67	5	3.82 Hybrid regime
115	Jordan	**3.93**	3.58	4.29	3.89	4.38	3.53 Authoritarian
116	ozambique	**3.85**	3.58	2.14	5	5	3.53 Authoritarian
	Kuwait	**3.85**	3.17	4.29	3.89	4.38	3.53 Authoritarian
118	anmar	**3.83**	3.67	3.93	3.89	5.63	2.06 Authoritarian
119	uritania	**3.82**	3	3.57	5	3.13	4.41 Authoritarian
120	Niger	**3.76**	5.25	1.14	3.33	4.38	4.71 Authoritarian
121	Comoros	**3.71**	4.33	2.21	4.44	3.75	3.82 Authoritarian

122	Nicaragua	3.63	2.67	1.86	3.89	5.63	4.12 Authoritarian
123	Angola	3.62	1.75	2.86	5.56	5	2.94 Authoritarian
124	Gabon	3.61	2.58	2.21	4.44	5	3.82 Authoritarian
125	Cambodia	3.59	1.33	5	2.78	5.63	3.24 Authoritarian
126	Algeria	3.5	2.58	2.21	3.89	5	3.82 Authoritarian
127	Egypt	3.36	3.58	3.21	3.33	3.75	2.94 Authoritarian
128	Ethiopia	3.35	0	3.57	5.56	5	2.65 Authoritarian
	Rwanda	3.35	1.67	5	2.78	4.38	2.94 Authoritarian
130	China	3.32	0	5	3.89	6.25	1.47 Authoritarian
131	Republic of the Congo	3.31	3.17	2.5	3.89	3.75	3.24 Authoritarian
132	Cameroon	3.28	3.17	2.86	3.33	4.38	2.65 Authoritarian
133	Qatar	3.19	0	4.29	2.22	5.63	3.82 Authoritarian
134	Zimbabwe	3.16	0.5	2	4.44	5.63	3.24 Authoritarian
	Venezuela	3.16	1.67	1.79	4.44	4.38	3.53 Authoritarian
136	Guinea	3.14	3.5	0.43	4.44	4.38	2.94 Authoritarian
137	Belarus	3.13	0.92	2.86	3.89	5.63	2.35 Authoritarian
138	Togo	3.1	3.17	0.79	3.33	5	3.24 Authoritarian
139	Vietnam	3.08	0	3.21	3.89	5.63	2.65 Authoritarian
140	Oman	3.04	0	3.93	2.78	4.38	4.12 Authoritarian
141	Eswatini	3.03	0.92	2.86	2.22	5.63	3.53 Authoritarian
142	Cuba	3	1.08	3.57	3.33	4.38	2.65 Authoritarian
143	Afghanistan	2.97	2.92	1.14	4.44	2.5	3.82 Authoritarian
144	Kazakhstan	2.94	0.5	2.14	4.44	4.38	3.24 Authoritarian
	Russia	2.94	2.17	1.79	5	2.5	3.24 Authoritarian
146	Djibouti	2.87	0.42	1.79	3.89	5.63	2.65 Authoritarian
147	United Arab Emirates	2.76	0	3.93	2.22	5	2.65 Authoritarian
148	Bahrain	2.71	0.83	3.21	2.78	4.38	2.35 Authoritarian
149	Azerbaijan	2.65	0.5	2.14	3.33	3.75	3.53 Authoritarian

Rank	Country	Score	Electoral process and plura-lism	Functioning of government	Political partici-pation	Political culture	Civil liber-ties	Regime type
150	Iran	2.45	0	3.21	4.44	3.13	1.47	Authoritarian
151	Eritrea	2.37	0	2.14	1.67	6.88	1.18	Authoritarian
151	Laos	2.37	0.83	2.86	1.67	5	1.47	Authoritarian
153	Burundi	2.33	0	0.43	3.89	5	2.35	Authoritarian
154	Libya	2.19	1	0.36	1.67	5	2.94	Authoritarian
155	Sudan	2.15	0	1.79	2.78	5	1.18	Authoritarian
156	Uzbekistan	2.01	0.08	1.86	2.22	5	0.88	Authoritarian
157	Guinea-Bissau	1.98	1.67	0	2.78	3.13	2.35	Authoritarian
158	Yemen	1.96	0	0	3.89	5	0.88	Authoritarian
159	Saudi Arabia	1.93	0	2.86	2.22	3.13	1.47	Authoritarian
159	Tajikistan	1.93	0.08	0.79	1.67	6.25	0.88	Authoritarian
161	Equatorial Guinea	1.92	0	0.43	3.33	4.38	1.47	Authoritarian
162	Turkmenistan	1.72	0	0.79	2.22	5	0.59	Authoritarian
163	Chad	1.61	0	0	1.67	3.75	2.65	Authoritarian
164	Central African Republic	1.52	2.25	0	1.11	1.88	2.35	Authoritarian
165	Democratic Republic of the Congo	1.49	0.5	0.71	2.22	3.13	0.88	Authoritarian
166	Syria	1.43	0	0	2.78	4.38	0	Authoritarian
167	North Korea	1.08	0	2.5	1.67	1.25	0	Authoritarian

The Democracy Index has been criticized for lacking transparency and accountability beyond the numbers. To generate the index, The Economist Intelligence Unit has a scoring system in which various experts are asked to answer 60 questions and assign each reply a number, with the weighted average deciding the ranking. However, the final report does not indicate what kinds of experts, their number, whether the experts are employees of the Economist Intelligence Unit or independent scholars, or the nationalities of the experts.

Our focus is our position and we are looking at the most advanced democracy and this tables gives us a clear picture and Nigeria must move up and this is achievable and I would like us to remain positive and believe in our institutions, if really we are moving to the next level as promised by the government of the day, electoral process must improve and we must take the bull by the horn. Most times there are incidents of logistics problems, materials

arriving late. These problems affect the vote casting or absence of officials and many more challenges like ballot boxes box was snatched.

The Chairman, Independent National Electoral Commission (INEC) Prof. Mahmood Yakubu while addressing an emergency session in Abuja before the 2019 general elections said that the timetable was "no longer feasible." He said this after widespread reports of problems with the delivery of election materials, including ballot papers. He continued in his address that the delay was necessary to give the commission time to address vital issues and "maintain the quality of our elections", but did not provide further details.

"We must improve our process of ballot and results collations during an election and these results will be adjudged free and fair and all stakeholders will be satisfied at the end of the day".

Prof. Mahmood Yakubu (INEC chairman).

(INEC to adopt electronic voting in 2019, daily post newspaper, May 25 2016)

The issue of security during an election is another challenge, most polling units has no police officials are deployed despite the huge amount of monies are allocated. During the last gubernatorial election in Anambra State, last The Nigerian police force demanded for 1 Billion Naira for providing security although this was reduced to 300 million Naira, this is rather too much and if one might ask, how many policemen were deployed to Anambra?, we must learn to put the interest of our nation first before our own selfish interest.

We are aware that the policemen were not enough and states like Rivers State had to use military. Some public analysts claimed that its because the state was perceived to be too volatile and police cannot handle situations should crises erupt. Such insinuations should stop as it does no one any good.

The electoral personnel mostly members of the National Youths' Service Corps (NYSC) were owed their allowances and the affected corps member refused to work. This led to the process of accreditation of voters not commencing in good time when all material was on ground.

There were also issues of violence and snatching of ballot boxes, this is evident when we decide to use ballot papers, and this makes an election end up with litigations at designated tribunals.

There were also cases of the card readers not reading PVC cards of some voters at Sabon Gari in kano State , these people could not cast their votes and also the biometrics of some voters could not be done as well and some other polling units the card reader refuse to function. This was a disaster and the law says that a voter cannot vote if the accreditation was not done and some part of the northern parts of the country voted, this was a source of confusion and INEC has a lot of issues to resolve.

With the present electoral system we run in Nigeria encourages corruption to a large extent, most stakeholders will want to exploit the situation and inflate budgets , we spent over 240 billion on 2019 election, this is outrageous and we must be ready to adopt a cost effective system which is the focus of this book.

Among the first 20 nations with best democratic index, Germany used e-voting and stopped the process, I want to believe that stakeholders are responsible for this action and will use this opportunity to stress that the success of any system depends on the stakeholders like political parties, law makers , regulatory body – INEC, voters etc. they must accept the idea, support its implementation and execution and we will not have need for the tribunals or minimize the job of this legal juggernauts. At the moment we have several cases that emanated from the 2019 elections these cases are ongoing.

Rigging has been an age long practice all over the world and we must allow election malpractices take over our system.

On February 23, 2019, Nigeria witnessed another broader electoral cycle with the conduct of the presidential and national assembly elections by the independent electoral commission. According to INEC, 34.75% representing a total number of 28,614,190 cast their votes. This number represents 0.91% less than the number of total registered voters of 84,004,084.

What this implies that people are doubtful about the country's electoral process and don't bother about the characters of persons contesting elective positions. They also seem not to care about what becomes of Nigeria's democracy in the future.

The youths that are successful in the private sector, should be involved in politics and ensure they bring their wealth of experience to serve the nation. This is to end the perception that our process is usually marred with all kinds of fraud and no one sees anything good in this process.

There were also allegations of some incumbent governors using mercenaries to vote for them and their anointed candidate during elections, these allegations happened in Imo, Kano state. These are credibility issues, I recall during the run-off elections in Kano some strange faces were noticed at Gwarzo, the locals raised alarm but the security agents could not handle the situation and these elements were allowed to cast their votes.

E-voting, will ensure that there's sanity in our electoral process, encourage more people to participate, improve the country's democratic index and ensure that right choices of candidates are made.

We are fully aware that e-voting cannot prevent some other challenges like vote buying and inducements, the concerned authorities , Civil liberties organizations have put in efforts to educate the electorate , this is not our focus in this book , championing improved processes is our main focus.

During research, I have come to discover that many Nigerians are concerned about the stress at the polling stations, violence, failed technologies and this discourages massive turnout during elections; this will not allow the right choices of candidates to be made. The Borno State collation agent for the Peoples Democratic Party(PDP) in the last presidential election, Mr. Nicholas Msheliza, has said that the total votes of 911,786 declared by the Independent National Electoral Commission (INEC) were well over the accredited voters across the state. According to him, 'Virtually all the results sheets that were brought to the state collation centre were mutilated...There was virtually no result sheet that was tendered at the state collation centre that did not have calculation error, and I did reject most of them...The Returning Officer of the first respondent (INEC), would always ask the local government collation officers to go outside the collation centre to reconcile figures, add them up and when they tallied, they should come back to present them."

These were excerpts from the presidential election tribunal sitting in Abuja, though we don't know the authenticity of this testimony, but the perception is that elections in Nigeria are usually rigged. Collation of results is manual; this does not allow immediate release of results and improved process will curb all these issues, within 24 hours of an election results will be reeled out to the nation and winners declared immediately.

Chapter 2

Case study: Advanced Democracy in the World: review of processes

The dream for any true Nigeria democrat is dream is for our democracy to be the most developed in the world and this feat can be achieved. As a nation we need to embrace excellence and stop giving excuses that our democracy is still evolving, the need to embrace robust processes cannot be over emphasized, if really we are fighting corruption we should not engage in sharp practices like rigging, falsifying result sheets etc. , thus our democratic index can improve from 108th position and we join the league of best democracies in the world, Each and every Nigerians are the ones that will make this feat possible & achievable.

In this chapter we will look at 3 countries that are fully democratic; they are Norway, Switzerland and Brazil. We want to see the e-voting concepts in these countries, review the challenges and its successes.

Norway

Norway is a parliamentary democracy and constitutional monarchy. The country is governed by a prime minister, a cabinet, and a 169-seat parliament that is elected every four years and cannot be dissolved. Free and fair elections to the multiparty parliament were held in 2009.

"It's very strange not to vote" says the 18-year-old, as if stating the painfully obvious. "It's like a normal thing".

This assertion by this young adult, is because the electoral process is not complex and very convenient, I'm sure our people will say what do you expect from an advanced society, United states was downgraded in this index and we need to find out why electioneering in this country is the best all over the world.

There are eight political parties in Norway's legislature — instead of just Republicans and Democrats — and the system means none of them can gain power alone. Instead they must try to build coalitions with enough support to form a government.

"You have a lot of cooperation between parties in Norwegian politics ... and the political debate climate is much milder than in the U.S," according to Carl Knutsen, a politics professor at the University of Oslo. "

The attitude of the politicians matters a lot, definitely these 8 political parties are not at war in occupying positions , no matter the party that gets an upper hand, national government is usually formed to ensure all parties are involved and represented, this shows that if processes must be seen as effective, the political parties must form part of the success by ensuring there is cooperation, unity, national interest comes first before our selfish interest and thus service to our mother land must be paramount in our hearts.

The Norwegian electoral system is based on the principles of direct election and proportional representation in multi-member electoral divisions. Direct election means that the electors vote directly for representatives of their constituency by giving their vote to an electoral list. Proportional representation means that the representatives are distributed according to the relationship to one another of the individual electoral lists in terms of the number of votes they have received. Both political parties and other groups can put up lists at elections.

In the case of parliamentary elections, the country is divided into 19 constituencies corresponding to the counties, including the municipal authority of Oslo which is a county of its own. The number of members returned to the Storting is 169. The number of members to be returned from each constituency depends on the population and area of the county, each inhabitant counts one point, while each square kilometre counts 1.8 points. Of the 169 members returned, 150 are elected as constituency representatives while 19, one seat from each constituency, are elected as members at large. All electoral offices run for 4 years and the king is responsible for fixing a date for the election, usually in September.

The Constitution has several fundamental provisions relating to parliamentary elections. These apply to such matters as the conditions for entitlement to vote and disfranchisement, the number of members of the Storting and the allocation of these to the counties, the method of election, the criteria for eligibility, and review of the validity of the election. The detailed provisions relating to the conduct of elections, to the Storting, to county councils and to municipal councils, are to be found in the Representation of the People Act 2002 (Act No. 57 of 28 June 2002). In addition, Regulations have been issued with further provisions in certain areas.

Any person entitled to vote must be included in a municipal register of electors on Election Day. The register of electors is a list of persons in the municipal authority area who are entitled to vote. The electors are entered in the register of electors in the municipal authority area where they were registered with a residential address on 30 June in the year of election. Any person who has been resident outside Norway for a continuous period exceeding 10 years, must apply for inclusion in the register of electors in the municipal authority area in which the person in question was last registered as being resident. This does not apply to those who are members of the diplomatic corps or the consular service or are part of their households.

The Register is pasted in the public for the electorate to ensure that their names are on the register and cases of omission would be reported to the electoral committee for correction.

Polling normally takes place in the following manner:

1) The elector goes to a polling booth where the act of voting shall be performed in a secluded room and unobserved.

2) The elector takes the ballot paper of the party or group for which he or she wishes to vote and makes any changes that he or she might wish.

3) The elector folds the ballot paper so that nobody can see how he or she has voted and goes to an election official, who stamps the ballot paper.

4) The elector then puts the ballot paper into the ballot box.

Any person who votes shall be crossed off in the register of electors. The election official checks that the elector has been included in the register of electors and that he or she has not been crossed off as having already voted. The elector shall produce proof of identity if he or she is not known to the election official. The crossing off in the register of electors must take place before electors put their ballot papers into the ballot box.

The results are collated at different municipal and the results released, this is the same system we run in Nigeria, the only difference is that Norway runs a monarchy system; Though Norway had experimented e-voting during elections held in 2011 and 2013. But the trials were suspended because voters' fears about their votes becoming public could undermine democratic processes. Political controversy and the fact that the trials did not bring about a massive turnout, also led to the experiment ending. In a statement, Norway's Government Office of Modernisation said it was ending the experiments following discussions in the nation's parliament about efforts to update voting systems.

The statement said although there was "broad political desire" to let people vote via the net, the poor results from the last two experiments had convinced the government to stop spending money on more trials. The 2013 trial was also controversial because immediately prior to the election, criticism was levelled at the encryption scheme used to protect votes being sent across the net. Software experts called for the entire voting system to be rewritten to better protect data.

A report looking into the success of the 2013 trial said about 70,000 Norwegians took the chance to cast an e-vote. This represented about 38% of all the 250,000 people across 12 towns and cities that were eligible to vote online. The concerns here is that Norwegians will not want their vote to be made public but rather will prefer a secret ballot and they are not comfortable with the data encryption schemes been adopted, they believe there can be manipulation of their votes and the experiments have since ended. This implies that e-voting is not in use in Norway.

The report by Norway's Institute of Social Research also expressed worries about the fact that online voting took place in what it called "uncontrolled environments". This, it said, undermined the need for a vote to be made in secret without anyone influencing the voter as they made their choice.

Switzerland

The Swiss parliament has two chambers, the National Council and the Council of States. In the National Council, the cantons are represented according to population. In the Council of States, each canton has two representatives, but there are also a few half-cantons with one representative each. For the National Council, there are uniform electoral rules for the country at large; for the Council of States, it is up to each canton to determine the electoral rules if they are democratic.

Switzerland's Executive, Judicial and Legislative institutions are organized on federal, cantonal and communal levels. Switzerland, unlike many of other European states, does not have a President or a Prime Minister, and the country's citizens are at the pinnacle of power. The Federal Council holds the executive power and is composed of seven power-sharing Federal Councillors elected by the Federal Assembly. The judicial branch is headed by the Federal Supreme Court of Switzerland, whose judges are elected by the Federal Assembly. Switzerland has a tradition of direct democracy.

Apart from low turnout, national elections in Switzerland have also been claimed as the least 'nationalised' elections in Western Europe (Caramani 2004). Party support and turnout have been found to be highly regionalised, Which suggests, according to the literature on the nationalisation of politics (See

Schattschneider[1960] [1997], Stokes [1976]), that voters have been reacting to local rather than to national political stimuli in terms of parties, candidates, and issues.

The parliament elects the president, a representative and does not have powers, the people have more powers, it's a peculiar kind of democracy in the whole of Europe, this implies that the elections are basically parliamentary; the lower and upper chambers. Though our concern is the process of elections, the elections are only parliamentary elections.

But in fact, this election is mainly about electing a government. The seven-member Federal Council is elected by parliament (not directly by the people), so clearly the political make-up of parliament is crucial – the parties with the most seats have the best chance of winning places in the Council.

Switzerland is introducing e-voting step-by-step. The principle of

"security before speed" applies. Currently two systems are being used: the system developed in the canton of Geneva, which is also being used by other cantons; and the e-voting system used in the canton of Neuchâtel, which was developed by Swiss Post. The Swiss e-voting system was locally developed and was used in the last election and they planned to involve hackers to determine possible cracks in the system.

In a public intrusion test, Swiss Post will allow hackers to legally attack its e-voting system from February 25 to March 24. The goal is to improve the system's security. As of Thursday, nearly 2,000 hackers had registered their external link to participate in the test: with 26% in Switzerland, 15% in France, 7% in the United States and 5% in Germany.

Over the past 15 years several cantons have used e-voting on a trial basis with systems developed by Swiss Post or canton Geneva. Many Swiss voters – especially those living abroad – are eager to vote online.

A major flaw was found in Swiss voting online system, A cryptographic trap door could let someone change votes cast using Switzerland's online Vote system without being detected. The specific issue is the way the system receives and counts votes before shuffling them and anonym zing voter details (everyone provides a birth date and an initialization code). Once they've been shuffled, the votes are counted and then decrypted. The trap door means someone could switch all the legitimately cast ballots for fraudulent ones, undetected.

The software vendor SCYTL, provides electronic voting services to over 35 countries, including the United States. It says it's working to fix the flaw, but the fact that it managed to creep into the system in the first place is worrying. And researchers say they've still only tested a fraction of the code base. It's one of many issues uncovered with online and electronic voting.

Critics of electronic voting, including popular security analyst Bruce Schneier, note that "computer security experts are unanimous on what to do (some voting experts disagree, but it is the computer security experts who need to be listened to; the problems here are with the computer, not with the fact that the computer is being used in a voting application)... DRE machines must have a voter-verifiable paper audit trails... Software used on DRE machines must be open to public scrutiny" to ensure the accuracy of the voting system. Verifiable ballots are necessary because computers can and do malfunction, and because voting machines can be compromised.

Brazil

Brazilian election laws are very complex and detailed. The law requires that all candidates who hold executive positions resign six months before the election (see The Legislature, this ch.). No "write-in" candidacies are allowed; only candidates officially presented by a registered political party may participate. Parties choose their candidates in municipal, state, or national conventions. Although the legislation does not recognize party primaries officially, on occasions they have been used informally.

Voting is considered both a right and a duty in Brazil; thus, registration and voting are compulsory between the ages of eighteen and seventy. Illiterates vote, but their voting registration card identifies their status, and they sign the voting list with a fingerprint on election day.

Elections are done on the national level for the president and legislature. The president is elected to a four-year term by absolute majority vote through a two-round system. The National Congress (Congresso Nacional) has two chambers. The Chamber of Deputies (Câmara dos Deputados) has 513 members, elected to a four-year term by proportional representation. The Federal Senate (Senado Federal) has 81 members, elected to an eight-year term, with elections every four years for alternatively one-third and two-third of the seats. Brazil has a multi-party system, with such numerous parties that often no one party has a chance of gaining power alone, and so they must work with each other to form coalition governments.

E-voting has been used for their elections since 1996, they have developed the system, with the first tests carried out in the state of Santa Catarina. The primary design goal of the Brazilian voting machine is extreme simplicity, the model being a public phone booth.

The Brazilian voting machine accomplishes three steps (voter identification, secure voting and tallying) in a single process thereby eliminating fraud based on forged or falsified public documents. Political parties have access to the voting machine's programs before the election for auditing.

The first Brazilian voting machines were developed in 1996 by a Brazilian partnership of three companies Omnitech (previously known as TDA), Microbase and Unisys do Brasil attending the TSE RFP for the Brazilian Elections in 1996. This machine was a modified IBM PC 80386 compatible clone, known as UE96. In 1998, Diebold-Procomp, Microbase and Samurai (formerly known as Omnitech) partnered to produce UE98. In 2000, Microbase and Diebold-Procomp developed the UE2000 together. In 2000, Brazil completed the first completely automated election.

The original operating system was VirtuOS, like DOS and includes multitasking support, was developed by Microbase. It was used in the 1996, 1998 and 2000 elections. In 2002, Unisys was unable to renew their partnership with Microbase, and was unable to reuse the VirtuOS based code. Microsoft stepped in and provided licenses Windows CE operating system free of charge. In 2008, another initiative from the TSE Electronic voting team migrated to a Linux (dubbed UEnux) OS to reduce costs and take full control of development cycle. It was incorrectly reported by the press that the UEnux project was carried out by Diebold/Procomp.

There remain some questions about the security of the electronic voting system, but no case of election fraud has been uncovered:

Critics argue that the voting machines do not produce receipt for the voter, nor maintain an internal paper-based journal which would allow for vote auditing. This makes them highly dependent on trusting the software. The application program which verifies the internal integrity of the system is itself vulnerable to modification. An inspection by the City of StoEstevão, Bahia described the system of seals and closure of the machine as simple and allowed easy access to the internal memory slot. It is possible to violate the secrecy of the vote, obtaining the list of the Voter registry IDs and the order of the votes. So, by simple comparison one could determine which ID voted for which candidate.

Election workers could vote in place of absent voters without their permission. However, voting sections are composed of multiple workers drawn at random from the population as a means of preventing this type of fraud.

On the eve of an election, the election authorities in each State select a number of voting machines by lot (all available voting machines take part in that lot, identified by their serial number), and those machines so selected, instead of being used in actual pooling stations, are retained in the seat of the State's Regional Electoral Court for a "parallel voting", conducted for audit purposes in the presence of representatives designated by the political parties. The audit vote takes place on the same date as the election. This parallel voting is a mock election but the votes entered in the voting machine are not secret, instead they are witnessed by all party representatives present at the audit process. The whole audit is filmed, and the representatives of the political parties present for the audit direct publicly that a random quantity of votes are to be inserted in the machine for each candidate.

A tally is kept of the instructions received from each party representative. Each party representative orders a number of votes to be inserted at the machine, but he/she only reveals that number, and the recipients, during the audit. So, the numbers are not previously known, because the only way they could be known by others is if there was collusion between rival parties. At the end of the process, then, when all the parties have directed that certain number of votes then chosen are to be registered for each candidate in the audit vote, the votes ordered to be inserted by each party representative for each candidate are added up, and the total number of votes of the mock election is known, as well as the total number of votes of each candidate. Once the mock votes end and the profile of the vote is known, the electronic counting of the votes contained in the voting machines used during the audit takes place. The result indicated by the voting machines software has to correspond to the previously known result.

Brazil has successfully implemented the e-voting and introduced methodology of audit and as described above , the process is filmed and all the political parties are involved in the audit trail, the only concern of most countries using the automated system is the security of the system, vulnerabilities that could lead to compromise of the votes casted & collation, some countries have continued the experiments for several years all in a bid to obtain a perfect system, let us look at a snapshot of e-voting all over the world.

Brazil, India, Estonia and Belgium are the countries that have fully implemented e-voting since 1996, 1982 and 1999 respectively. They have never reported hacking of data or compromise of data; they keep on enhancing the EVM machines as required.

Legislation is required before acquisition and implementation; the electoral laws of the land must be in place before venturing into it. India commenced e-voting since 1982, they have had improvements since then and there approach it's the best as an audit trail is done to ensure the correctness of the vote cast unlike most systems that does not allow audit, they now print details of vote cast per ward or constituencies for the party agents to cross check and agree, this would give it more credibility.

Electoral process in most countries is with ballot papers, most countries are also ensuring they introduce e-voting because this will increase the turnout and participation of voters and also ensure that collation of result is done within 24 hours. This will make electioneering convenient and credibility at the polls can be guaranteed.

Norway has been testing her e-voting software for 15 years, they had to employ hackers all over the world to break into the system, this according to the developers will allow them know the loop holes, ensure updates are carried out to address the issues , a whopping 150,000USD was invested for this task. Convectional or automated system can be compromised, man has always seek for was to take advantage of any electoral system by manipulating for selfish gains. Electoral fraud is not only peculiar to Africa but all over the world and this has to be eliminated as much as possible so the wish of the electorate can be fulfilled or I might say, so that votes will count and most importantly the integrity of such exercise can be achieved.

All voting systems face threats of some form of electoral fraud. The types of threats that affect voting machines vary. Research at Argonne National Laboratories revealed that a single individual with physical access to a machine, such as a Diebold Accuvote TS, can install inexpensive, readily available electronic components to manipulate its functions.

Other examples include; tampering with the software of a voting machine to add malicious code that alters votes to favour a certain candidate .Multiple groups has demonstrated this possibility.

Private companies manufacture these machines. Many companies will not allow public access or review of the machines source code, claiming fear of exposing trade secrets. Tampering with the hardware of the voting machine to alter vote totals or favour any candidate.

Some of these machines require a smart card to activate the machine and vote. However, a fraudulent smart card could attempt to gain access to voting multiple times or be pre-loaded with negative votes to favour one candidate over another, as has been demonstrated. Abusing the administrative access to the machine by election officials might also allow individuals to vote multiple times.

Election results that are sent directly over the internet from the polling place centre to the vote-counting authority can be vulnerable to a man-in-the-middle attack, where they are diverted to an intermediate website where the man in the middle flips the votes in favour of a certain candidate and then immediately forwards them on to the vote-counting authority. All votes sent over the internet violate the chain of custody and hence should be avoided by driving or flying memory cards in locked metal containers to the vote-counters. For purposes of getting quick preliminary total results on election night, encrypted votes can be sent over the internet, but final official results should be tabulated the next day only after the actual memory cards arrive in secure metal containers and are counted. Most countries make use of transparent boxes; this has not prevented stuffing the box with ballot papers that are fake.

Although I agree that technology cannot prevent other electoral virus like vote buying, Inducements, violence, Demography manipulation etc., this can be addressed by continuous voters' education, though it's not our focus in this book.

E-voting across the internet might not be credible after all, hackers can compromise this system if there is no adequate security for the database , network infrastructure , citizens in diaspora can participate by casting their votes online and more voters participation is guaranteed , for countries that don't prefer the offline machines must ensure that the security of these infrastructures are protected using relevant tools and it must be reviewed and tested regularly to ensure it's actually protected.

Country	Technology currently used in elections		Year of introduction	Notes
	Natio nal	Munici pal		
Austra lia	No	Some	2001	During the 2007 federal election, electronic voting was made available for blind and low-vision persons. Since 2001, in Australian Capital Territory elect ions and since 2015 in New South Wales state elections.
Switzerland				Internet voting for expatriates only from 2014
United Arab Emirates	Yes			
United Kingdom	No			Used for central counting of ballots in Scotland from 2007
United States of America	Yes	No		
Venezuela	Yes		1998	

Netherlands	No		1990s	Discontinued 2007
Norway	No	No	n/a	Trialled 2003
Philippines	Yes	Yes	2010	Currently in review by Congress due to technical glitches, defective vote-counting machines, SD cards and transparency issues.
Romania				Limited trial 2003
South Korea				For central counting of ballot papers only
Spain	No	No		

Table: Implementation of e-voting worldwide,

Source: Wikipedia

Chapter 3

Future of electoral process in Nigeria

Nigeria, most populous black nation in the world and once regarded as the giant of Africa, we have been improving with respect to electoral process. We must agree that our process is bewildered with irregularities like rigging, integrity of results, and poor distribution of materials across the wards nationwide and most importantly excessive expenditures during elections.

Democracy is regarded as a 'way of life' interrelated with the perceptions and assumptions, common experiences of individuals and it is about living together. So, it can be stated that democracy is not a static concept but a dynamic, active and changing process.

Democracy is based on faith in the dignity and worth of every single individual as a human being.... The object of a democratic education is, therefore, the full, all-round development of every individual's personality. ... i.e. an education to initiate the students into the many-sided art of living in a community. It is obvious, however, that an individual cannot live and develop alone. ... No education is worth the name which does not inculcate the qualities necessary for living graciously, harmoniously and efficiently with one's fellow men.

Uncompromised electoral process can make the citizenry beat their chest and herald integrity of our polls; I agree technology without cooperation of the stakeholders cannot take us to the promise land. Technology has improved our way of life, why should we not use it to improve our electoral processes.

At this point we need to appreciate the introduction of the smartcard readers for voters authentication in 2015 elections, though many challenges were experienced then and in 2019 in most wards were the infrastructure was deployed and want to encourage the election umpire to seek for improvements and reduce downtime during elections, this takes care of voters authentication, this infrastructure will not be scrapped, it should be used for future election.

The 2019 elections ended in May and it would have been wise for the umpire and various stakeholders review the processes, take critical look at ways of improving the issues that occurred and this can help us in having a strong and virile democracy. The current administration's fight against corruption is commendable but it's not only when public funds are stolen alone but it should cover all spheres of life in our society. Electoral process should not be left out in this war, our dream society is that which is devoid of any kind of theft and manipulation.

The Senate recently passed the Electoral Act No. 6 2010 (Amendment) Bill 2017 into law. The passage of this Bill in the Senate is a bold, innovative and common-sense step on Electoral Reforms designed to guarantee free, fair and credible elections in Nigeria. Without much ado, these are some of the highlights of the Bill;

1) There shall now be full biometric accreditation of voters with Smart Card Readers and/or other technological devices, as INEC may introduce for elections from time to time.

2) Presiding Officers must now instantly transmit accreditation data and results from Polling Units to various collation centres. Presiding officer who

contravene this shall be imprisoned for at least 5 years (no option of fine).

3) All Presiding Officers must now first record accreditation data and polling results on INEC's prescribed forms before transmitting them. The data/result recorded must be the same with what they transmitted.

4) INEC now has unfettered powers to conduct elections by electronic voting.

5) manual registers, INEC is now mandated to keep Electronic registers of voters.

6) INEC is now mandated to publish voters' registers on its official website(s) for public scrutiny at least 30 days before a general election and any INEC staff that is responsible for this but fails to act as prescribed shall be liable on conviction to 6 months' imprisonment.

7) INEC is now mandated to keep a National Electronic Register of Election Results as a distinct database or repository of polling unit by polling unit results for all elections conducted by INEC.

8) Collation of election result is now mainly electronic, as transmitted unit results will help to determine final results on real time basis.

9) INEC is now mandated to record details of electoral materials – quantities, serial numbers used to conduct elections (for proper tracking).

10) A political party whose candidate dies after commencement of an election and before the declaration of the result of that election now has a 14-day window to conduct a fresh primary in order for INEC to conduct a fresh election within 21 days of the death of the party's candidate;

11) Political parties' Polling Agents are now entitled to inspect originals of electoral materials before commencement of election and any Presiding Officer who violates this provision of the law shall be imprisoned for at least1 year.

12) No political party can impose qualification/disqualification criteria, measures or conditions on any Nigerian for the purpose of

nomination for elective offices, except as provided in the 1999 Constitution.

13) The election of a winner of an election can no longer be challenged on grounds of qualification, if the he (winner) satisfied the applicable requirements of sections 65, 106,

131 or 177 of the Constitution of the Federal Republic of Nigeria, 1999 (as amended) and he is not, as may be applicable, in breach of sections 66, 107, 137 or 182 of the Constitution of the Federal Republic of Nigeria, 1999. [For example, a person's election cannot be challenged on the ground that he did not pay tax, as this is not a qualifying condition under the Constitution.]

14) All members of political parties are now eligible to determine the ad-hoc delegates to elect candidates of parties in indirect primaries. The capacity of party executives to unduly influence or rig party primaries has been reasonably curtailed, if not totally removed.

15) Parties can no longer impose arbitrary nomination fees on political aspirants. The Bill passed prescribes limits for each elective office as follows:

(a) One Hundred and Fifty Thousand Naira (N150,000) for a Ward Councillorship aspirant in the FCT;

(b) Two Hundred and Fifty Thousand Naira (N250,000) for an Area Council Chairmanship aspirant in the FCT;

(c) Five Hundred Thousand Naira (N500,000) for a House of Assembly aspirant;

(d) One Million Naira (N1,000,000) for a House of Representatives aspirant;

(e) Two Million Naira (N2,000,000) for a Senatorial aspirant;

(f) Five Million naira (N5,000,000) for a Governorship aspirant; and

(g) Ten Million Naira (N10,000,000) for a Presidential aspirant.

16. Relying on the powers of the National Assembly in Paragraph 11 of Part II (Concurrent Legislative List) of the Second Schedule (Legislative Powers) to the Constitution of the Federal Republic of Nigeria, 1999 (as amended), the Senate also passed measures reforming procedures regulating Local Government Elections. State Independent Electoral Commissions can no longer conduct elections that do not meet minimum standards of credibility.

17. Any INEC official who disobeys a tribunal order for inspection of electoral materials shall be imprisoned for 2 years, without an option of a fine.

Source: Daily Trust

The fourth item on the list says that INEC has the powers to conduct elections by electronic voting, this is our major interest in this book, and we will deal with it accordingly.

There are different types of e-voting systems, they are Punch-card, Optical scan, Direct-recording electronic, Internet, M3 EVM. Our focus will be on the M3 which is produced in India and it suits our environment considering some factors, we describe various approaches briefly.

Punch-card voting systems

With punch-card voting systems, the ballot is a card (or cards) and the voters punch holes in it (with a supplied punch device) next to their candidate or choice. After punching the hole(s), the voter may place the ballot in a ballot box, or the voter may feed the ballot into an electronic vote tabulating device at the voting place.

Two common types of punch-card voting systems are the "Votomatic" and the "Datavote" system. With the Votomatic card, the locations at which holes may be punched to indicate votes are each assigned numbers. The number of the hole is the only information printed on the card. The list of candidates or ballot issue choices and directions for punching the corresponding holes are printed in a separate booklet. With the Datavote card, the name of the candidate or description of the choice is printed on the ballot next to the location of the hole to be punched. The re-count of ballots in Florida during the 2000 presidential election created a debate about the reliability of punch-card voting systems. After 2000, the popularity of punch-card voting systems in the US decreased significantly.

Optical scan (voting) systems

These systems use an optical scanner to read and count marked ballot papers. Various systems can be defined as optical scan (voting) systems including mark sense systems whereby an optical mark (e.g. made with a graphite pencil on the ballot paper) can be recognized by a scanner electronic ballot markers (EBM) that can be used to fill out optical scan ballots. The systems look like traditional DREs, but they record votes on paper ballots instead of internal memory. EBM can aid a disabled voter in marking a paper ballot; it can allow for audio interfaces an example is:

Digital Pen: These systems use ballots on digital paper. A small camera in the pen is able to recognize where the voter marks the digital ballot paper. The ballots are collected in the polling station and the digital pen has to be returned to the elections staff for tabulation. Optical scan voting systems combine paper with electronic devices. All the systems keep a tangible ballot paper which serves as a tangible record of the voter's intent. By that, optical scan systems allow for manual recounts of ballots. The big advantage is that the counting process can be done in a central place and that the counting is much faster. The system is easily understandable by the voter: for him/her it doesn't really change much; they can still mark their preference on a ballot paper. And if – for whatever reason – the scanning system fails to work, ballots can be counted manually.

Direct-recording electronic (DRE) voting machines

With a DRE machine, voting can be done on Election Day or it can be used as an advance voting device in polling stations. It is easily understandable: the voter just pushes a button next to his/her favourite candidate or choice. Or the DRE machines have a touch screen displaying the ballot. After the election or referendum, the DRE machine produces a tabulation of the voting data stored in a removable memory component and/or as printed copy. The system may also allow for transmission of individual ballots or vote totals to a central location. The result can then be consolidated in one central place.

DRE voting machines started to be massively used in 1996 in Brazil. They were also used on a large scale in the US after the Florida 2000 experience. Vision-impaired voters benefit from DRE machines because they can cast their vote without help from another person. DRE machines were also deployed in Europe, e.g. in the Netherlands, where the company NEDAP provided their own DRE machines since 1989. They were used in the Netherlands until 2006. In 2009, the German Constitutional Court found that the DRE-type voting machines used in parliamentary elections in Germany were unconstitutional since they did not allow citizens to examine the determination of the result.

Internet voting

Internet voting refers to the use of the Internet to cast and/or transmit the vote. Internet voting can take various forms depending on whether it is used in uncontrolled environments (remote Internet voting) or not (Polling Site Internet Voting, Kiosk Voting). With remote Internet voting neither the client machines nor the physical environment are under the control of election officials. Voters can cast their vote at practically any place (at home, at the workplace, at public Internet terminals etc.). The vote is then transmitted over the Internet. This method offers the most advantages to voters, but at the same time it suffers from them most security concerns. They include doubts about the Internet as a means of transmission of confidential information, fear of hacker attacks and anxiety about the possibility of undue influence being exerted on the voter during the voting process (e.g. 'family voting').

The other options (polling site Internet voting or kiosk voting) refer to systems where voters cast their ballot from client machines that are physically situated in official polling stations or in public places that are controlled by election officials. In both cases, hardware and software components are controlled by election officials. The difference is that with polling site Internet voting the authentication of the voters may take place by traditional means and with kiosk voting (in public places), the physical environment and voter authentication are not directly under control of election officials

M3 EVM Machine

We are also aware of infrastructure gap in Nigeria, most rural areas do not have stable electricity, and this would affect the use of the M3 EVM machines.

EVM machines that work over the network are quite vulnerable and open to attacks as mentioned earlier, what we need is an offline EVM machine and this is manufactured in India and Namibia has taken delivery of these machines for their general elections.

The Indian electronic voting machine(EVM) were developed in 1989 by Election Commission of India in collaboration with Bharat Electronics Limited and Electronics Corporation of India

Limited. The Industrial designers of the EVMs were faculty members at the Industrial Design Centre, IIT Bombay. The EVMs were first used in 1982 in the by-election to North Paravur Assembly Constituency in Kerala for a limited number of polling stations.

EVM consists of two units, a control unit, and the balloting unit. The two units are joined by a five-meter cable. Balloting unit facilitates voting by a voter via labelled buttons while the control unit controls the ballot units, stores voting counts and displays the results on 7 segment LED displays. The controller used in EVMs has its operating program etched permanently in silicon at the time of manufacturing by the manufacturer. No one (including the manufacturer) can change the program once the controller is manufactured. The control unit is operated by one of the polling booth officers, while the balloting unit is operated by the voter in privacy. The officer confirms the voter's identification then electronically activates the ballot unit to accept a new vote. Once the voter enters the vote, the balloting unit displays the vote to the voter, records it in its memory. A "close" command issued from the control unit by the polling booth officer registers the vote, relocks the unit to prevent multiple votes. The process is repeated when the next voter with a new voter ID arrives before the polling booth officer.

EVMs are powered by an ordinary 6 volt alkaline battery, manufactured by Bharat Electronics Limited, Bangalore and Electronics Corporation of India Limited, Hyderabad. This design enables the use of EVMs throughout the country without interruptions because several parts of India do not have the power supply and/or erratic power supply. The two units cannot work without the other. After a poll closes on a particular election day, the units are separated and the control units moved and stored separately in locked and guarded premises.

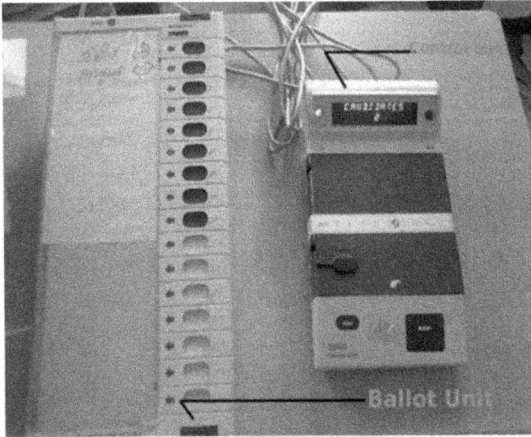

Both units have numerous tamper-proof protocols. Their hardware, by design, can only be programmed once at the time of their manufacture and they cannot be reprogrammed. They do not have any wireless communication components inside, nor any internet interface and related hardware. The balloting unit has an internal real-time clock and a protocol by which it records every input-output event with a time stamp whenever they are connected to a battery pack. The designers intentionally opted for battery power, to prevent the possibility that the power cables might be used to interfere with the reliable functioning of an EVM.

An EVM can record a maximum of 3840 (now 2000) votes and can cater to a maximum of 64 candidates. There is provision for 16 candidates in a single balloting unit and up to a maximum of 4 balloting units with 64 candidate names and the respective party symbols can be connected in parallel to the control unit.[32] If there are more than 64 candidates, the conventional ballot paper/box method of polling is deployed by the Election Commission. After a 2013 upgrade, an Indian EVM can cater to a maximum of 384 candidates plus "None of the above" option (NOTA).

The current electronic voting machines in India are the M3 version with VVPAT capability, the older versions being M1 and M2. They are built and encoded with once-write software (read-only masked memory) at the state-owned and high-security premises of the Bharat Electronics Limited and the Electronics Corporation of India Limited.[6][35] The inventory of election EVMs is securely tracked by the Election Commission of India on a real-time basis with EVM Tracking Software (ETS). This system tracks their digital verification identity and physical presence. The M3 EVMs has embedded hardware and software that enables only a control unit to work with a voting unit issued by the Election Commission, as another layer of tamper-proofing. Additional means of tamper proofing the machines include several layers of seals. Indian EVMs are stand-alone non-networked machines.

How is it used?

The control unit is with the presiding officer or a polling officer and the balloting Unit is placed inside the voting compartment. The balloting unit presents the voter with blue buttons (momentary switch) horizontally labelled with corresponding party symbol and candidate names. The Control Unit, on the other hand, provides the officer-in-charge with a "Ballot" marked button to proceed to the next voter, instead of issuing a ballot paper to them. This activates the ballot unit for a single vote from the next voter in the queue. The voter must cast his vote by once pressing the blue button on the balloting unit against the candidate and symbol of his choice.

As soon as the last voter has voted, the Polling Officer-in-charge of the Control Unit will press the 'Close' Button. Thereafter, the EVM will not accept any votes. Further, after the close of the poll, the Balloting Unit is disconnected from the Control Unit and kept separately. Votes can be recorded only through the Balloting Unit. Again the Presiding officer, at the close of the poll, will hand over to each polling agent present an account of votes recorded. At the time of counting of votes, the total will be tallied with this account and if there is any discrepancy, this will be pointed out by the Counting Agents. During the counting of votes, the results are displayed by pressing the 'Result' button. There are two safeguards to prevent the 'Result' button from being pressed before the counting of votes officially begins. (a) This button cannot be pressed till the 'Close' button is pressed by the Polling Officer-in-charge at the end of the voting process in the polling booth. (b) This button is hidden and sealed; this can be broken only at the counting centre in the presence of designated office.

Though we have good testimonies of this machine, it is advisable that we conduct mock elections and put it to test before adopting it for the general election, investing in this is worthwhile so that our umpire and stakeholders can have a feel and get used to its workability and implementation before roll out in the next general election. Alternatively, we have some governorship elections that come up before the general election, Kogi State, Bayelsa State, Edo State and Osun State Gubernatorial elections can be used as testing ground.

What are the benefits

The benefits of this machine are enormous, and they are as follows;

- Elimination of printing ballot papers.

- Cost of Logistics – transportation of election would stop.

- Elections can start in good time and unnecessary delays can be avoided.

- Cost of organizing elections will reduce.

- EVMs will be kept and warehoused by INEC State headquarters.

- Lack of power in our rural areas will not affect Its deployment.

- The machines are offline, not to any network.

- Casted votes are done on the microchip in the machine and cannot be compromised, hijacked or stolen.

- Hardware based solution that cannot be manipulated by any party.

- Hackers cannot break into the system.

- Collation of results can be done in good time.

- Audit trails can be generated on paper for party agents to review and agree with other parties.

- If the machine is vandalized, the microchip can be recovered and records of casted votes can be recovered. Manufacturers of the EVMs have developed a Totalizer unit which can connect several balloting units and would display only the overall results.

- No snatching of ballot boxes and rigging.

- Reduced or elimination of litigation at election tribunals.

Security

Manufacturers of Electronic Voting Machines, namely Electronics Corporation of India Limited, Hyderabad and Bharat Electronics Limited, Bengaluru have said that EVMs are "unhackable" and tamper-proof as programming for EVMs is done at a secure manufacturing facility in ECIL and BEL (where operations are logged electronically) and not with chip manufacturers. Control and ballot units in EVMs and VVPATs have an anti-tamper mechanism by which they become non-operational if it is illegally opened. EVMs are standalone machines, have no radio frequency transmission device features, operate on battery packs and cannot be reprogrammed. The control Unit of EVMs has a real-time clock that logs every event on its right from the time it was switched on. The anti-tamper mechanism in the machine can detect even 100-millisecond variations.

Verifiable Audit trails

Election Commission of India appointed an expert technical committee headed by Prof. P. V. Indiresan (former Director of IIT-M) when at an all-party meeting majority of political parties backed the proposal to have a VVPAT in EVMs to counter the charges of tampering. The committee was tasked to examine the possibility of introduction of a paper trail so that voters can get a printout that will show symbol of the party to which the vote was cast. After studying the issue, the committee recommended introduction of VVPAT system.

Election Commission accepted Prof. Indiresan committee's recommendations and decided to conduct field trials of the system.

Field trials of the VVPAT system were conducted for some local elections in 2 pollen stations and the exercise was successful. This upgrade is available on the machine and it gives credibility to the votes cast by allowing an audit trail to be produced by the equipment.

The Election Commission on 19 January 2012 agreed to add a "paper trail" of the vote cast. The upgrade of EVMs that followed modified the EVM software and a printer was attached to the machine. With the VVPAT system, when a vote is cast, it is recorded in its memory and simultaneously a serial number and vote data is printed out. This states that Anil Kumar, the managing director of the state-owned EVM manufacturer Bharat Electronic Limited, ensures more confidence in the voting results. The printouts, Kumar said, "are used later to cross-check the voting data stored in the EVMs". Voter-verifiable paper audit trail was first used in an election in India in September 2013 in Noksen in Nagaland. The EVM made in India is the most suitable for our environment and already it has been exported to Nepal, Bhutan, Namibia and Kenya.

Cost & Benefit Analysis

Just concluded 2019 elections , =N=242 billion naira was budgeted , =N=36 billion estimated for cost of ballot papers and boxes , =N=85 billion for logistics which involves transportation of materials and personnel , this amounts to =N=121 billion , 50% of the entire budget and this expenditures continue to grow due to inflation in the economy , automating the elections will reduce these costs drastically and on the long run the elections would become cheaper to organize and ambiguity associated with the elections in the past will be removed and the electorate will be rest assured of the integrity of the polls & this will encourage high turnout of voters in all elections.

What is the cost of the made in India EVM , M3 EVM goes for 17,000 Rupees per unit , that's about 89,752.79 Naira and we have 119,973 pollen units in Nigeria , this implies that we need about 10.7 billion naira to acquire these machines, there are other associated cost which is not included and compared to budget of printing ballot papers that is 36 billion naira and this will help us reduce cost of organizing elections significantly, also ensure the polls are credible.

Chapter 4

National Interest

The M3 EVM has been recommended by the author and the very important step is the endorsement of the amended electoral reform bill by the executive and I believe this will be done soon , this bill has many reforms and the only aspect concerning us is the 'powers vested on INEC to organise elections using electronic voting'.

I want to commend the 8th assembly for coming up with this reforms and also ensuring its passed and my wish is that it doesn't end up like the PIB bill that has been passed for more than 16 years and it has not seen the light of the day.

Acquiring the M3 is not an issue for our great nation Nigeria but its implementation is key to its success and the stakeholder must be actively involved in this area. We appreciate that this machine was invented in 1982 and has undergone series of improvements, stakeholders have been actively involved based on concerns and issues raised by political parties, electoral umpire and modifications have been achieved by the manufacturers.

As a nation we should adopt technology in every sphere of our national lives , this will not only eliminate waste of resources but ensure we have a system that could be adjudged as having integrity and also encourage potential users of such technologies and enthrone confidence in our public institutions, this will definitely improve our democratic index.

We need to remain positive as citizens of Nigeria, it's not strange to us that advanced societies are compared with us, they also passed through challenges at early stage and improved with time. We must believe in our nation and our public institutions that they can deliver corporate goals of our country.

INEC must be commended for innovations and it's active involvement in voters education, they must do more in this light if e-voting is introduced eventually, lectures on the use must be delivered in different local languages so as to ensure the electorate in the rural communities are not left out, this must be done, statistics show that there are more voters in the rural areas than urban areas.

Non Governmental Organisations (NGO's) should also get involved, complementing the efforts of INEC is of essence and should be taken seriously, let's not just criticize but also render support in educating the rural electorate during the roll out of any technology that will be adopted in the future.

We must acknowledge that technology can fail, this often happens when there is no stakeholder buy-in and refusal to adopt standard implementation techniques, thus the people can determine success or failure and we should not rule out sabotage and as a true Nigerian we should not allow this, because processes must improve in our country and this will definitely make us proud.

Electronic voting can be a success in Nigeria, once the right technology is adopted , successfully implemented and let us careless about countries that has made attempts and it failed and countries that have been testing for more than a decade, let's remain positive and focused.

About the Author

Dr. Alex Ndukwe is a 1993 graduate of computer science, University of Nigeria Nsukka (UNN), he holds a Master's degree in Business Administration from the Ambrose Alli University, Ekpoma and a Doctorate degree in Computer science, Atlantic international university, Florida, United states of America.

He also holds the following certifications; ITIL V3- Foundations, ITIL service Operations V3, COBIT 5, ISO 20000 – Foundation, ISO 20000 Practitioner.

Dr. Alex worked at Indo-Nigerian Bank Limited for 11years and Sterling bank plc for 12 years, managing ICT infrastructures and user support, Northern Region.

Currently, he is the CEO of Tekville Systems, an ICT firm based at Abuja, FCT.